EMMANUEL JOSEPH

The Weightless Compass, Navigating Life with Curiosity, Creativity, and Calm

Copyright © 2025 by Emmanuel Joseph

All rights reserved. No part of this publication may be reproduced, stored or transmitted in any form or by any means, electronic, mechanical, photocopying, recording, scanning, or otherwise without written permission from the publisher. It is illegal to copy this book, post it to a website, or distribute it by any other means without permission.

First edition

This book was professionally typeset on Reedsy. Find out more at reedsy.com

Contents

1	Chapter 1: The Journey Begins	1
2	Chapter 2: The Power of Curiosity	3
3	Chapter 3: The Creative Spirit	5
4	Chapter 4: The Calm Mind	7
5	Chapter 5: Balancing Curiosity, Creativity, and Calm	9
6	Chapter 6: Embracing Change with Curiosity	11
7	Chapter 7: Cultivating Creativity in Everyday Life	13
8	Chapter 8: Finding Calm in a Busy World	15
9	Chapter 9: The Role of Intuition	16
10	Chapter 10: The Art of Letting Go	17
11	Chapter 11: Building Resilience	18
12	Chapter 12: The Power of Gratitude	19
13	Chapter 13: The Magic of Moments	20
14	Chapter 14: The Power of Connection	21
15	Chapter 15: Embracing Vulnerability	22
16	Chapter 16: The Journey of Self-Discovery	23
17	Chapter 17: The Weightless Compass in Action	24

1

Chapter 1: The Journey Begins

In the journey of life, we often seek direction, a sense of purpose, and the means to navigate through our days with grace and intention. This book is our compass, guiding us to explore the depths of curiosity, creativity, and calm. Imagine a compass that weighs nothing, effortlessly guiding us through the complexities of existence. This weightless compass isn't just an instrument, but a mindset, a way of perceiving the world with a light and open heart. As we embark on this journey, we'll discover that the keys to a fulfilling life lie in the balance between these three elements.

Curiosity is the spark that ignites our sense of wonder and drives us to explore the unknown. It's the fuel for lifelong learning, pushing us to ask questions, seek answers, and never settle for the status quo. In this chapter, we'll delve into the importance of curiosity, how it shapes our perceptions, and how we can cultivate it in our everyday lives. By embracing curiosity, we open ourselves up to a world of possibilities and continuous growth.

Creativity, on the other hand, is the expression of our inner thoughts, emotions, and imagination. It's the art of turning our ideas into reality, whether through writing, painting, cooking, or problem-solving. Creativity allows us to connect with our true selves and the world around us in meaningful ways. In this chapter, we'll explore the power of creativity, how it influences our lives, and practical tips for nurturing our creative spirit. Through creativity, we find joy, purpose, and a sense of accomplishment.

Calm is the foundation that grounds us, allowing us to navigate life's challenges with resilience and grace. It's the ability to remain centered amidst chaos, to find peace within ourselves, and to approach situations with a clear mind and a compassionate heart. In this chapter, we'll discuss the significance of calm, how it impacts our well-being, and techniques for cultivating a calm and mindful mindset. By embracing calm, we build inner strength and create a harmonious life.

As we journey through this book, we'll explore the interconnectedness of curiosity, creativity, and calm, and how they work together to shape our lives. Each chapter will provide insights, stories, and practical exercises to help you navigate your unique path with a weightless compass. So, let's begin this adventure together, and discover the transformative power of living with curiosity, creativity, and calm.

2

Chapter 2: The Power of Curiosity

Curiosity is the driving force behind every great discovery and innovation. It's the spark that ignites our sense of wonder and propels us to explore the unknown. In this chapter, we'll delve into the importance of curiosity and how it shapes our perceptions of the world. We'll explore the role of curiosity in personal growth, problem-solving, and creativity. By embracing curiosity, we open ourselves up to a world of possibilities and continuous learning.

Curiosity fuels our desire to learn and grow. It pushes us to ask questions, seek answers, and challenge the status quo. When we approach life with a curious mindset, we become more open-minded and adaptable. We see the world through a lens of possibility and wonder, and we're more willing to take risks and explore new ideas. In this chapter, we'll discuss the benefits of curiosity and how it can enhance our personal and professional lives.

Curiosity also plays a crucial role in creativity. When we're curious, we're more likely to experiment, take risks, and think outside the box. We're more open to new experiences and ideas, and we're more willing to embrace failure as a learning opportunity. In this chapter, we'll explore the connection between curiosity and creativity, and how we can cultivate a curious mindset to fuel our creative endeavors.

Cultivating curiosity requires intentional effort and practice. It's about being open to new experiences, asking questions, and seeking out opportunities to learn and grow. In this chapter, we'll provide practical tips for nurturing curiosity in our everyday lives. By embracing curiosity, we can unlock our full potential and create a life filled with wonder, exploration, and growth.

3

Chapter 3: The Creative Spirit

Creativity is the expression of our inner thoughts, emotions, and imagination. It's the art of turning our ideas into reality, whether through writing, painting, cooking, or problem-solving. In this chapter, we'll explore the power of creativity and how it influences our lives. We'll discuss the benefits of creativity, how it shapes our perceptions, and practical tips for nurturing our creative spirit.

Creativity allows us to connect with our true selves and the world around us in meaningful ways. It gives us a sense of purpose and fulfillment, and it helps us navigate life's challenges with resilience and grace. When we engage in creative activities, we tap into our inner wisdom and intuition, and we find joy in the process of creation. In this chapter, we'll explore the different forms of creativity and how they impact our well-being.

The creative process is a journey of exploration and discovery. It's about experimenting, taking risks, and embracing failure as a learning opportunity. In this chapter, we'll discuss the stages of the creative process and how we can cultivate a creative mindset. We'll provide practical tips for overcoming creative blocks, finding inspiration, and staying motivated in our creative pursuits.

Creativity is not limited to the arts; it can be applied to every aspect of our lives. Whether we're solving a problem at work, finding a new way to approach a task, or coming up with a fun activity for our family, creativity plays a crucial role. In this chapter, we'll explore how we can infuse creativity into our everyday lives and create a life filled with joy, purpose, and fulfillment.

4

Chapter 4: The Calm Mind

Calm is the foundation that grounds us, allowing us to navigate life's challenges with resilience and grace. It's the ability to remain centered amidst chaos, to find peace within ourselves, and to approach situations with a clear mind and a compassionate heart. In this chapter, we'll discuss the significance of calm and how it impacts our well-being. We'll explore techniques for cultivating a calm and mindful mindset.

A calm mind is essential for our mental and emotional well-being. It allows us to stay focused, make better decisions, and respond to stress with resilience. When we're calm, we're more in tune with our inner wisdom and intuition, and we're better able to navigate life's challenges with grace. In this chapter, we'll discuss the benefits of a calm mind and how it influences our overall well-being.

Cultivating calm requires intentional effort and practice. It's about finding ways to quiet the mind, reduce stress, and stay present in the moment. In this chapter, we'll provide practical tips for creating a calm and peaceful environment, managing stress, and practicing mindfulness. By embracing calm, we can build inner strength and create a harmonious life.

Calm is not about avoiding challenges or difficult emotions; it's about finding balance and inner peace amidst the chaos. In this chapter, we'll explore how we can cultivate a calm mindset and approach life's challenges with resilience and grace. We'll provide techniques for staying grounded, managing emotions, and finding peace within ourselves. By embracing calm, we can navigate life with a clear mind and a compassionate heart.

5

Chapter 5: Balancing Curiosity, Creativity, and Calm

The interplay between curiosity, creativity, and calm is a delicate dance that shapes our lives. When we find harmony among these three elements, we unlock our full potential and create a life of fulfillment and joy. In this chapter, we'll explore how to balance curiosity, creativity, and calm, and how they complement each other in our daily lives. We'll discuss the benefits of this balance and provide practical tips for achieving it.

Curiosity fuels our desire to explore and learn, while creativity allows us to express our discoveries in meaningful ways. Calm, on the other hand, provides the foundation that grounds us, enabling us to navigate our journey with resilience and grace. When we cultivate curiosity, creativity, and calm, we create a dynamic and harmonious life. In this chapter, we'll discuss the interconnectedness of these elements and how they work together to shape our perceptions and experiences.

Finding balance requires intentional effort and practice. It's about being mindful of our thoughts and actions, and creating space for each element in our lives. In this chapter, we'll provide practical tips for balancing curiosity, creativity, and calm. We'll explore techniques for staying curious, nurturing our creative spirit, and cultivating a calm and mindful mindset. By finding harmony among these elements, we can create a life filled with joy, purpose, and fulfillment.

6

Chapter 6: Embracing Change with Curiosity

Change is an inevitable part of life, and our ability to navigate it with curiosity can determine our success and happiness. In this chapter, we'll explore the role of curiosity in embracing change and how it can help us adapt and thrive in new situations. We'll discuss the benefits of approaching change with a curious mindset and provide practical tips for cultivating curiosity during times of transition.

Curiosity allows us to see change as an opportunity for growth and learning. When we approach change with an open mind and a sense of wonder, we become more adaptable and resilient. In this chapter, we'll discuss the importance of staying curious during times of change and how it can help us navigate uncertainty with confidence. We'll provide practical tips for maintaining a curious mindset, seeking out new experiences, and embracing the unknown.

Change often brings challenges and uncertainty, but it also offers opportunities for growth and transformation. In this chapter, we'll explore how curiosity can help us overcome fear and resistance to change. We'll discuss the benefits of staying curious and open-minded, and provide techniques for navigating change with resilience and grace. By embracing change with curiosity, we can create a life filled with new possibilities and continuous growth.

7

Chapter 7: Cultivating Creativity in Everyday Life

Creativity is not limited to the arts; it can be infused into every aspect of our lives. In this chapter, we'll explore how we can cultivate creativity in our everyday activities and create a life filled with joy and fulfillment. We'll discuss the benefits of creativity, how it shapes our perceptions, and practical tips for nurturing our creative spirit in our daily routines.

Creativity allows us to see the world through a fresh lens and find innovative solutions to problems. When we engage in creative activities, we tap into our inner wisdom and intuition, and we find joy in the process of creation. In this chapter, we'll explore the different forms of creativity and how they impact our well-being. We'll provide practical tips for infusing creativity into our daily lives, whether through cooking, gardening, or finding new ways to approach tasks.

The creative process is a journey of exploration and discovery. It's about experimenting, taking risks, and embracing failure as a learning opportunity. In this chapter, we'll discuss the stages of the creative process and how we can cultivate a creative mindset in our everyday lives. We'll provide techniques for finding inspiration, staying motivated, and overcoming creative blocks. By nurturing our creative spirit, we can create a life filled with joy, purpose, and fulfillment.

8

Chapter 8: Finding Calm in a Busy World

In today's fast-paced world, finding calm can be challenging, but it's essential for our well-being. In this chapter, we'll explore techniques for cultivating calm and mindfulness in our daily lives. We'll discuss the importance of creating a peaceful environment, managing stress, and staying present in the moment. By embracing calm, we can build inner strength and create a harmonious life.

A calm mind allows us to stay focused, make better decisions, and respond to stress with resilience. When we're calm, we're more in tune with our inner wisdom and intuition, and we're better able to navigate life's challenges with grace. In this chapter, we'll discuss the benefits of a calm mind and how it influences our overall well-being. We'll provide practical tips for creating a calm and peaceful environment, managing stress, and practicing mindfulness.

Cultivating calm requires intentional effort and practice. It's about finding ways to quiet the mind, reduce stress, and stay present in the moment. In this chapter, we'll explore techniques for staying grounded, managing emotions, and finding peace within ourselves. We'll discuss the importance of self-care and provide practical tips for incorporating calming practices into our daily routines. By embracing calm, we can create a life of balance and inner peace.

9

Chapter 9: The Role of Intuition

Intuition is a powerful tool that guides us in making decisions and navigating life's challenges. It's the inner voice that whispers to us, offering insights and wisdom beyond logic and reasoning. In this chapter, we'll explore the role of intuition and how it influences our lives. We'll discuss the benefits of trusting our intuition, how it shapes our perceptions, and practical tips for tapping into our inner wisdom.

Intuition allows us to connect with our true selves and the world around us in meaningful ways. It helps us make decisions that align with our values and purpose, and it guides us toward fulfilling experiences. In this chapter, we'll discuss the importance of trusting our intuition and how it can enhance our personal and professional lives. We'll provide practical tips for listening to our inner voice, tuning into our intuition, and making decisions with confidence.

Cultivating intuition requires intentional effort and practice. It's about being present, quieting the mind, and paying attention to our inner signals. In this chapter, we'll explore techniques for developing and strengthening our intuitive abilities. We'll discuss the importance of mindfulness, self-reflection, and creating space for inner listening. By embracing intuition, we can navigate life with greater clarity and purpose.

10

Chapter 10: The Art of Letting Go

Letting go is an essential part of personal growth and transformation. It's the process of releasing what no longer serves us, whether it's limiting beliefs, negative emotions, or past experiences. In this chapter, we'll explore the art of letting go and how it can lead to greater freedom and fulfillment. We'll discuss the benefits of letting go, how it shapes our perceptions, and practical tips for embracing this practice.

Letting go allows us to create space for new possibilities and experiences. It frees us from the burdens of the past and opens us up to a future filled with potential. In this chapter, we'll discuss the importance of letting go and how it can enhance our well-being. We'll provide practical tips for releasing limiting beliefs, forgiving ourselves and others, and moving forward with a sense of liberation.

The process of letting go requires intentional effort and practice. It's about acknowledging our emotions, accepting our experiences, and choosing to release what no longer serves us. In this chapter, we'll explore techniques for letting go, including mindfulness, self-compassion, and creating new narratives. By embracing the art of letting go, we can create a life filled with freedom, joy, and fulfillment.

11

Chapter 11: Building Resilience

Resilience is the ability to bounce back from challenges and setbacks with strength and grace. It's the quality that allows us to navigate life's ups and downs with a positive and determined mindset. In this chapter, we'll explore the importance of resilience and how it influences our lives. We'll discuss the benefits of building resilience, how it shapes our perceptions, and practical tips for cultivating this essential quality.

Resilience allows us to face challenges with confidence and determination. It helps us stay grounded and focused, even in the face of adversity. In this chapter, we'll discuss the importance of resilience and how it can enhance our personal and professional lives. We'll provide practical tips for developing resilience, including mindfulness, self-care, and creating a supportive network.

Building resilience requires intentional effort and practice. It's about developing a positive mindset, finding meaning in our experiences, and nurturing our inner strength. In this chapter, we'll explore techniques for building resilience, including goal-setting, self-reflection, and embracing change. By cultivating resilience, we can navigate life's challenges with grace and determination.

12

Chapter 12: The Power of Gratitude

Gratitude is a powerful practice that can transform our lives and bring us greater happiness and fulfillment. It's the act of recognizing and appreciating the good in our lives, no matter how small. In this chapter, we'll explore the power of gratitude and how it influences our well-being. We'll discuss the benefits of practicing gratitude, how it shapes our perceptions, and practical tips for incorporating this practice into our daily lives.

Gratitude allows us to see the beauty and abundance in our lives. It helps us focus on the positive and cultivate a sense of contentment and joy. In this chapter, we'll discuss the importance of gratitude and how it can enhance our personal and professional lives. We'll provide practical tips for practicing gratitude, including journaling, mindfulness, and expressing appreciation to others.

The practice of gratitude requires intentional effort and consistency. It's about making a conscious choice to focus on the positive and appreciate the good in our lives. In this chapter, we'll explore techniques for cultivating gratitude, including daily reflections, gratitude exercises, and creating a gratitude ritual. By embracing the power of gratitude, we can create a life filled with happiness, fulfillment, and abundance.

13

Chapter 13: The Magic of Moments

Life is made up of moments, both big and small, that shape our experiences and memories. In this chapter, we'll explore the magic of moments and how we can embrace them with curiosity, creativity, and calm. We'll discuss the importance of being present, savoring the beauty of everyday moments, and creating meaningful experiences. By embracing the magic of moments, we can create a life filled with joy and fulfillment.

Moments of joy, connection, and wonder are what make life truly meaningful. When we approach life with curiosity, creativity, and calm, we're more likely to notice and appreciate these moments. In this chapter, we'll discuss the importance of being present and mindful, and how it can enhance our well-being. We'll provide practical tips for savoring the beauty of everyday moments, finding joy in the little things, and creating meaningful experiences.

Creating meaningful moments requires intentional effort and practice. It's about being present, cultivating gratitude, and finding joy in the process of living. In this chapter, we'll explore techniques for embracing the magic of moments, including mindfulness, self-reflection, and creating rituals. By embracing the magic of moments, we can create a life filled with joy, wonder, and fulfillment.

14

Chapter 14: The Power of Connection

Connection is a fundamental aspect of the human experience. It's the bonds we form with others that give our lives meaning and fulfillment. In this chapter, we'll explore the power of connection and how it influences our well-being. We'll discuss the benefits of cultivating meaningful relationships, how they shape our perceptions, and practical tips for building and nurturing connections.

Meaningful connections allow us to feel seen, heard, and valued. They provide us with a sense of belonging and support, and they enrich our lives in countless ways. In this chapter, we'll discuss the importance of cultivating meaningful relationships and how they can enhance our personal and professional lives. We'll provide practical tips for building and nurturing connections, including active listening, empathy, and creating shared experiences.

Building meaningful connections requires intentional effort and practice. It's about being present, showing empathy, and investing time and energy into our relationships. In this chapter, we'll explore techniques for building and nurturing connections, including effective communication, creating rituals, and finding common ground. By embracing the power of connection, we can create a life filled with love, support, and fulfillment.

15

Chapter 15: Embracing Vulnerability

Vulnerability is the willingness to show up and be seen, even when it feels uncomfortable. It's the courage to be authentic and open, and to embrace our imperfections. In this chapter, we'll explore the power of vulnerability and how it can lead to greater connection and fulfillment. We'll discuss the benefits of embracing vulnerability, how it shapes our perceptions, and practical tips for cultivating this essential quality.

Embracing vulnerability allows us to connect with others on a deeper level. It helps us build trust and intimacy in our relationships, and it fosters a sense of belonging and acceptance. In this chapter, we'll discuss the importance of vulnerability and how it can enhance our personal and professional lives. We'll provide practical tips for embracing vulnerability, including self-compassion, authenticity, and creating a safe space for open communication.

Cultivating vulnerability requires intentional effort and practice. It's about being honest with ourselves and others, and embracing our imperfections with compassion. In this chapter, we'll explore techniques for embracing vulnerability, including self-reflection, mindfulness, and creating supportive relationships. By embracing vulnerability, we can create a life filled with authenticity, connection, and fulfillment.

16

Chapter 16: The Journey of Self-Discovery

Self-discovery is the process of exploring and understanding our true selves. It's the journey of uncovering our values, passions, and purpose, and aligning our lives with our authentic selves. In this chapter, we'll explore the journey of self-discovery and how it influences our well-being. We'll discuss the benefits of self-discovery, how it shapes our perceptions, and practical tips for embarking on this transformative journey.

Self-discovery allows us to connect with our true selves and create a life that aligns with our values and purpose. It helps us make decisions that resonate with our authentic selves, and it guides us toward fulfilling experiences. In this chapter, we'll discuss the importance of self-discovery and how it can enhance our personal and professional lives. We'll provide practical tips for embarking on the journey of self-discovery, including self-reflection, mindfulness, and seeking out new experiences.

The journey of self-discovery requires intentional effort and practice. It's about being curious, open-minded, and willing to explore new aspects of ourselves. In this chapter, we'll explore techniques for self-discovery, including journaling, meditation, and seeking out opportunities for growth. By embracing the journey of self-discovery, we can create a life filled with authenticity, purpose, and fulfillment.

17

Chapter 17: The Weightless Compass in Action

As we come to the end of our journey, it's time to put the weightless compass into action. In this chapter, we'll explore how to integrate curiosity, creativity, and calm into our daily lives and create a life filled with joy, purpose, and fulfillment. We'll discuss practical tips for applying the principles of the weightless compass, and how to navigate life's challenges with grace and intention.

Living with curiosity, creativity, and calm allows us to approach life with an open heart and a clear mind. It helps us stay grounded and focused, even in the face of adversity. In this chapter, we'll discuss the importance of integrating these principles into our daily lives and how they can enhance our well-being. We'll provide practical tips for staying curious, nurturing our creative spirit, and cultivating a calm and mindful mindset.

Integrating the principles of the weightless compass requires intentional effort and practice. It's about being present, staying curious, and embracing the journey of life with an open heart. In this chapter, we'll explore techniques for putting the weightless compass into action, including goal-setting, self-reflection, and creating rituals. By embracing the weightless compass, we can create a life filled with joy, purpose, and fulfillment.

As we conclude this book, remember that the journey of life is an ongoing process of exploration and discovery. Embrace the weightless compass and navigate your path with curiosity, creativity, and calm. May you find joy, purpose, and fulfillment in every moment, and create a life that aligns with your true self.

Book Description:

In a world often dominated by chaos and uncertainty, "**The Weightless Compass: Navigating Life with Curiosity, Creativity, and Calm**" offers a refreshing perspective on living a fulfilling and meaningful life. This insightful guide presents a unique approach to navigating life's complexities by embracing the harmonious interplay of curiosity, creativity, and calm.

Through seventeen thoughtfully crafted chapters, this book explores the transformative power of curiosity, the boundless potential of creativity, and the grounding influence of calm. Each chapter delves into these essential elements, providing readers with practical tips, inspiring stories, and actionable exercises to integrate these principles into their daily lives.

From cultivating a curious mindset and unleashing your creative spirit to finding inner peace and building resilience, "The Weightless Compass" is your companion on the journey of self-discovery and personal growth. Discover how to embrace change with an open heart, create meaningful moments, and nurture authentic connections. This book is an invitation to explore the magic of everyday life and create a path that aligns with your true self.

Whether you're seeking to enhance your well-being, ignite your passions, or simply find more joy in the present moment, "The Weightless Compass" offers valuable insights and guidance. Let this weightless compass guide you toward a life of curiosity, creativity, and calm, and unlock the limitless possibilities that await.

www.ingramcontent.com/pod-product-compliance
Lightning Source LLC
LaVergne TN
LVHW010445070526
838199LV00066B/6208